T0278038

Mr. Murphy, A Most Heavenly Cat
© 2024 Bonnie Donnelly

ISBN 979-8-35095-864-5

Mr. Murphy

A Most Heavenly Cat

A True Story

Bonnie Donnelly

Contents

Thinking back to the beginning, things began to change during our annual family beach vacation in June of 2018.

Little Addison, a petite nine-year-old, seemed to drink lots of extra water and juice that week. Her parents thought it was due to the hot days in the sun and did not think much about it.

The next week, though, while going to daily soccer practice back at home, Addison complained off and on of her stomach hurting. This was unusual behavior for her. Her parents thought it might be from the extra exertion at practices, or just being tired from the hot sun. They were not alarmed.

A couple days later, during a regular lunch date with her two older cousins, two older sisters and, me, Gram, at our favorite restaurant, that Addison's life quickly changed forever.

This calm, happy little girl who never caused a ripple had been unusually quiet until our lunch came. When I glanced over at her and our eyes met, she could not hold it in any longer and began to cry in real distress.

Troubled by her fearful tears, my instincts took over. I knew she was in real danger with pain. Thankfully, her elder cousin had also driven to the restaurant, so I told her to take the others home. I immediately left with Addison to the nearest Quick Care facility that happened to be just across the intersection from the restaurant.

Upon rapid examination, the doctor quickly did a urine test that revealed the problem to him. Without giving us the reason, we were instructed to get to the ER right away. We had a very anxious ride to the city hospital emergency room where she was further evaluated.

Time moved quickly and we were on our way via emergency transportation to the Children's Hospital in Columbus, Ohio.

As circumstances would have it, Addison's mother's business flight had just touched down in Dallas, Texas where she was to attend meetings that week. Upon getting the news about Addison, she quickly arranged for, and was provided a seat on the next flight back to Columbus.

For Addison's father, this was to have been a typical summer afternoon of yard work while the girls were with Gram. Fortunately, he was quick to join Addison at the Marietta ER for the medical transport to the Children's Hospital in Columbus, Ohio.

Upon arrival at the Hospital, things happened very rapidly, as if in a dream. Calm and friendly faces leaned into Addison on the ER cot. There was easy chit chat with her at the same time various equipment was turned on and being secured to her skin. It was apparent the medical team was well-practiced as the little beeps began a rhythm that gave this grandmother an invisible support hug.

Once the emergency medication took hold, (her A1C was thirteen at time of hospital admittance) it did not take long before she looked more comfortable, although she was very frightened of all that was going on around her as well as to her. There was an IV in one arm, monitor patches on her chest, and nurses were taking blood samples.

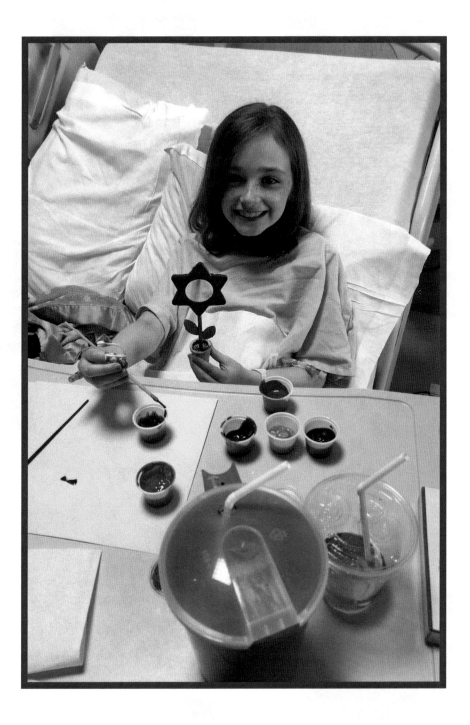

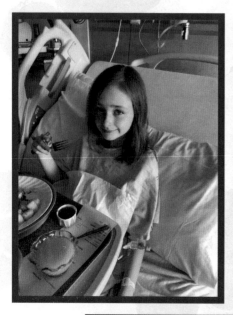

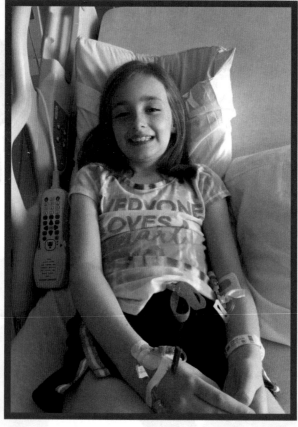

A distraction, though, was that through the afternoon, Addison was given as much bacon as she desired, and she loved bacon! Later we were told she was in desperate need of protein; so, bring on the bacon. For a nine-year-old, she weighed in at a slight fifty pounds.

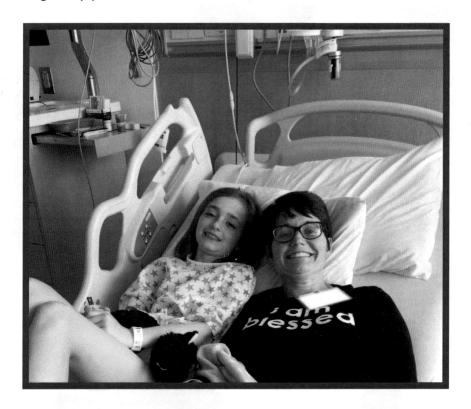

Fortunately, a parent was able to spend the nights with Addison during her hospitalization, and it was not long before she was back at home with a whole new daily routine.

Everything Old is New at Home

While Addison recovered in the hospital, her parents, her grandfather, and I received training to help administer the medicine she needed to live with Type 1 Diabetes. We also learned about the dangers of too many or too little doses. It is a precise measurement for her body.

For her, this means any food or drink that goes into her mouth must be evaluated for the number of carbohydrates. There is a particular mathematical calculation to determine whether or not she needs insulin.

This meant that for Addison, from then on, even a snack like a cookie or juice must be calculated with time of day, total carbo-hydrates of the food item, and her number level of glucose that is already in her system.

Many kitchen cupboard re-arrangements had to be made to accommodate her medical items.

An entire section was cleared for boxes of single-use syringes, cotton swabs, a battery operated glucose monitor, juice boxes on for when her glucose level needed quick elevation, and the tablets to check for ketones in her urine if her glucose level became too elevated.

There was also a shelf in the refrigerator kept especially for the precious insulin that Addison would need. Her body produced no insulin now. This was the beginning of her new life with Type 1 Diabetes.

Her parents had been given a direct phone number from her hospital doctor in case of an emergency. We kept daily charts in a binder notebook of her glucose numbers and carbohydrate counts from the foods she ate.

Besides the medication storage and the notebook information, Addison's dad hung a big chalk board on the wall beside the pantry where everyone could track and time her insulin needs. This changed daily, of course, but was a major help to remind us of important numbers.

The kitchen counter under the medication cabinet had the big notebook and the carry-bag that now went everywhere with Addison. It held her syringes, extra juice boxes, and the ketone meds. There was one more important item in that bag: an EpiPen of mediation should she go so low as to faint that could quickly go into a coma from her body's lack of insulin.

There is little notice that her body will run short of insulin or get too much glucose from food. These immediate items in her little backpack are needed wherever she goes to save her life.

Another part of Addison's new life was in planning for her needs at her elementary school. Her parents supplied an emergency kit for her at the office, where the school nurse, as well as the secretary and school principal, were trained to help.

She could still have the class birthday and special day treats like pizza; she just had to calculate and get an insulin shot beforehand.

Addison's days include calculating carbs to get the correct doses of insulin. There are various injection sites used to avoid the scar tissue that could interfere with the insulin coming into her under her skin.

Fast forward five years

She is a first-year student in high school. She now wears a sensor that attaches by a small conduit under her skin that communicates with an insulin pump that is also connected by a small indicator under her skin. These items "transmit" with each other. Addison has hand-held remotes to read her insulin levels. When she goes too low or too high in numbers, there is a beeping signal that she must give herself what she needs, be it water and walking to help flush too much glucose, or juice to elevate too low glucose.

These lifesaving monitors need their batteries changed every so many days to refresh insulin and to scan her glucose levels. So, there is regular checking of the cabinet inventory by her parents to keep supplies current.

Bye-bye BRACES!

When the insulin pump needs to be changed, it emits a beep sound every three days. The liquid insulin is in a small vial that she uses a syringe to get the dose amount from, then she inserts the syringe into the fresh pump that is attached to her skin.

The sensor needs to be changed every thirteen days. Addison has become very skilled at working with her devices that keep her alive. Should she neglect these things, she would become extremely sick, to the point of hospitalization and even death.

Living with Type 1 Diabetes is not a death knell, but it is a serious medical condition that needs constant checking.

So, Addison has several items with her wherever she goes, whether it be school, to the soccer fields, even while she sleeps.

One helpful part for her parents, though, is that the sensor is also synchronized to their cell phones. When her alarm goes off that she goes low in her sleep, for example, this alarm goes to their phones as well as Addison's should she need them.

Part Two: Mr. Murphy

We are a family of Christians. Our daughter, Addison's mother, keeps a morning tradition of devotions in a particular chair in the living room, that looks out the front porch window.

About two weeks after Addison's Columbus hospital stay, she was there in the middle of her study time when she glanced out to see a dirty-white cat peeking in at her.

Startled, she called Addison to see. Addison was delighted, of course, and immediately went for a bowl of milk and a towel as she headed for the back patio door.

It was not long before the cat was hungrily eating while being given the once over by mother and daughter. It was love at first sight.

Their successful plea to keep the kitten in the garage overnight gained time to get acquainted. Addison set up a lawn chair for herself and a blanket for the cat. The rest, as they say, is history.

After a visit to the veterinary for the needed checkup, and some family discussion, the orphan was adopted and named Mr. Murphy. Turns out he was a few months old, just undernourished. But he soon flourished into a gorgeous gentleman with one blue eye and one yellow eye, and a most beautiful, thick, white coat of the Turkish Angora.

Mr. Murphy became prince of the entire household. But the one person he spent the most time with was little Addison. He allowed her to carry him all over the place like a stuffed animal. He would drape over her shoulder, or cuddle in her lap. They were soon best friends.

Having a cat in the house might not seem unusual at all, but with Mr. Murphy around, things just feel better. He is a quiet guy, but at the same time, he loves to be in the middle of any activity that is happening in the house. He likes elevations. It is common to see him perched atop a kitchen counter, on a bookshelf, or anywhere else he can get a good vantage point.

Mr. Murphy likes to play hide and seek in any open cabinet, box, laundry basket or pantry. And yet, he is never far from the family. Once, when the chimney cleaners came, Murphy was right in the middle of the pile of vacuum hoses while sporting curious black streaks on his whiskers.

Or, when the house painters worked inside, Murphy was at home snooping around the ladders, wanting to climb up too.

There is always something happening with Murphy, but he is so extremely sweet. He is immediately forgiven for any mischief. He is particularly good, for example, at dissecting a lovely silk flower arrangement silently and completely from the dining room table. And he loves to carry little pieces of faux greenery around in his mouth like a jungle hunter proud of his prey.

It is when Addison needs TLC (tender loving care) that Mr. Murphy instinctively knows to get into action for her, to be close to her. It has been like this since the early days.

Even now, with five years of routine, Mr. Murphy remains ever near to his special friend.

Addison's story makes us believe that Mr. Murphy's appearance that day soon after her diagnosis was truly a divine gift. We are convinced it was and that Murphy is a true care giver to the entire family.

Addison's family and Mr. Murphy now live in South Carolina with Riley, an older black and white female cat who is usually found in the quiet upstairs bedroom area away from the hustle and bustle days. There is also a seventy-pound Berne Doodle, Birdie, who keeps Mr. Murphy company these days. Birdie watches over Addison on the rides to and from high school with dad, or any time at home when Mr. Murphy is on break.

Author's Note

Mr. Murphy and Addison's story may not seem unusual to pet lovers who understand the special devotion that often happens between pets and their families.

This is Addison's story that I witnessed personally since that first day at our little lunch. I have watched how they have relied on one another from their first day together.

May God bless all the children who live daily with difficult health conditions. And may God bless their pets who love them.

Birdie on duty sometimes for Mr. Murphy.